Welcome to
KIT'S WORLD
—— 1934 ——
Growing Up During America's Great Depression

THE AMERICAN GIRLS COLLECTION®

American Girl®

Printed in Malaysia
02 03 04 05 06 07 08 TWP 10 9 8 7 6 5 4 3 2 1
The American Girls Collection®, Kit®, Kit Kittredge®, and the
American Girl logo are trademarks of Pleasant Company.

Written by Harriet Brown
Edited by Tamara England
Designed and Art Directed by Will Capellaro,
Josh Mjaanes, Jane S. Varda, and Lynne Wells
Produced by Cheryll Mellenthin, Paula Moon, and Richmond Powers
Cover Illustration by Walter Rane and Jean-Paul Tibbles
Interior Illustrations by Philip Hood, Susan McAliley, Susan Moore,
Walter Rane, and Jean-Paul Tibbles
Illustration and Image Research by Rebecca Sample Bernstein,
Sally Jacobs, and Sally Wood
Photography by Jamie Young
Prop Research and Styling by Jean doPico
Permissions Coordination by Gail Longworth

Library of Congress Cataloging-in-Publication Data
Brown, Harriet, 1958–
Welcome to Kit's world, 1934 : growing up during America's Great Depression /
[written by Harriet Brown ; interior illustrations by Walter Rane . . . et al. ;
photography by Jamie Young].
p. cm.
Summary: Through photographs, illustrations, and both factual and fictionalized
anecdotes, shows what life was like in the United States during the Depression.
ISBN 1-58485-359-X
1. United States—Social life and customs—1918–1945—Juvenile literature.
2. United States—Social conditions—1933–1945—Juvenile literature.
3. Depressions—1929—United States—Juvenile literature.
4. Girls—United States—Social life and customs—20th century—Juvenile literature.
5. Girls—United States—Social conditions—20th century—Juvenile literature.
[1. United States—Social life and customs—1918–1945.
2. United States—Social conditions—1933–1945. 3. Depressions—1929—United States.
4. United States—History—1933–1945.]
I. Brown, Harriet, 1958– II. Rane, Walter, ill. III. Title.
E169.B8725 2002 973.917—dc21 2001036152

Table of Contents

Welcome to Kit's World

"These days a lot of things happen that aren't fair. There's no one to blame, and there's nothing that can be done about it." Charlie's voice sounded tired. "You better get used to it, Kit. Life's not like books. There's no bad guy, and sometimes there's no happily ever after, either."

— Valerie Tripp,
Meet Kit

In the 1930s, when Kit Kittredge was a girl, America had fallen into the terrible slippery hole of the Great Depression. It was a crisis so serious and widespread that almost every American was touched by it. Never before had so many Americans been without jobs, without money, without homes—and without hope. Like the Kittredges, some families escaped the hard times at first. But by 1932, the worst year of the Depression and the year Kit's story begins, the hard times had driven her father out of business, and the Kittredges were at risk of losing their home.

Kit is a fictional character. But the events and the time of her story are real. In fact, all the characters in Kit's world are drawn from the memories, letters, and diaries of real girls and boys and men and women from the 1930s.

Like Kit, girls growing up in the 1930s learned to be thrifty. They worked hard to help their families make ends meet. But life was not *all* hard work. Resourceful girls like Kit learned to have fun without spending money, and everyone appreciated and treasured what money *couldn't* buy—the kindness and generosity of family, friends, and even strangers.

In this book, you will travel back in time and imagine what it was like to live in Kit's world. You'll read about the hard times that girls like Kit and families like the Kittredges faced, and you'll see how they found ways to cope and rise above them.

The Roaring Twenties

Kit was born during the 1920s, a decade of high-flying *prosperity*, or good times, for many Americans. Business was booming. World War One was over, and Americans celebrated by having fun whenever they could. They went dancing. They went to the movies. They threw parties.

Style was everything. Young women called *flappers* started wearing short dresses and big fur-trimmed coats. They *bobbed* their hair, or cut it short. For the first time, many went to college and got jobs, so they could afford the new cars and radios that were being produced in America's factories.

If people didn't have money when they wanted something, they could buy on *credit*, or with borrowed money, and pay for it later. Few people believed that the good times wouldn't last.

FUN AND GAMES

Children shared in the good times, too. There were new dolls with eyes that closed, and that cried or said "Mama." There were puzzles, mechanical trains, and stuffed dogs that "barked." There were even shoes with springs attached for jumping!

This doll could talk when one of these blue cylinders was put into an opening in her back.

*Women read magazines like **Vogue** to keep up with all the latest styles and fashion news.*

YES SIR! THAT'S MY BABY

Words by Gus Kahn
Music by Walter Donaldson

Ain't We Got Fun

Irving Berlin, Inc.
MUSIC PUBLISHERS
1607 Broadway New York

Before everyone had radios, people bought sheet music so they could play and sing popular new songs at home.

A young flapper and her partner dance the Charleston, one of the wild new dances of the twenties.

Business Boom

Americans helped business grow in the 1920s by buying lots of new things, such as cars, appliances, and radios. These new products were affordable because the assembly line and mass production made them cheaper to make. People also helped businesses grow by buying stock in the companies that made these new products. A *share of stock* is a portion of ownership of a company, and the *stock market* is a system by which people buy and sell shares of stock. As the *economy*, or the system of making and buying goods, grows, so does the value of stocks, and investors can make a lot of money. By the mid-1920s, many people were investing in the stock market, hoping to grow rich. Some investors bought stock on credit, planning to repay their debts when stock prices increased.

But while investors' wealth was growing, workers' wages were not, and the economy was growing out of balance and becoming unstable. Then, in the late 1920s, business growth slowed, stock prices started to fall, and people started to lose money. Were the good times coming to an end?

AUTOMOBILE ASSEMBLY LINES
In 1913, it took 14 hours to put together a single automobile, and only wealthy people could afford one. By 1925, assembly lines turned out a new car every ten seconds. With mass production, one in every five Americans drove a car by the end of the 1920s.

*People supported companies by buying stock in them. They often received **stock certificates** as proof of their purchases.*

Cars got bigger and fancier as production methods improved.

CRASH!

The Great Depression officially began on October 29, 1929, a day known as Black Tuesday. On that day, people who had invested in stock—or shares of companies—panicked and began selling their shares. But because everyone wanted to sell all at once, the prices of stocks plummeted. Many people lost all their money that day in the great stock market "crash." Even people who hadn't invested in the stock market were affected when businesses closed and jobs were lost. The crash didn't cause the Depression all by itself, but it was one of a chain of events that brought America to its knees.

*The New York Stock Exchange, where stocks are bought and sold, is often referred to as **Wall Street**, because its main offices are located on Wall Street in New York City.*

Stock traders could track changes in stock values by reading paper "ticker tape" printouts.

Newsboys called out the headlines as they sold papers on the streets in the 1920s.

BROADWAY

SCREEN

VARIETY

PRICE 25¢

VOL. XCVII. No. 3   NEW YORK, WEDNESDAY, OCTOBER 30, 1929   88 PAGES

WALL ST. LAYS AN EGG

Dumb Is Deadly to Hostess Dance Hall Profesh

DROP IN STOCKS ROPES SHOWMEN

Kidding Kissers in Talkers Burns Up Fans of Screen's Best Lovers

Hunk on Winchell

When the Walter Winchells moved into 204 West 46th street, late last week, June, that's Mrs. Winchell, selected a special room as Walter's exclusive sleep den for his late hour nights. She situated the Winchell kidlets when her husband drove in at his usual eight o'clock the first morning to

Many Weep and Call Off Christmas Orders—Legit Shows Hit

MERGERS HALTED

The most dramatic event in the

Talker Crashes Olympus

Paris, Oct. 29.

Fox "Follies" and the Fox Movietone newsreel are running this week in Athens, Greece, the first sound pictures heard in the birthplace of world culture.

Boys who used to whistle and girls who used to giggle when love scenes were flashed on the screen are in action again. A couple of years ago they began to take the love stuff seriously and desired but the talkers are reviving the ha ha for film osculators.

Heavy loving lovers

BANK CLOSINGS

After the stock market crashed, hundreds of banks across the country closed their doors without warning, taking families' entire savings along with them. One farm family deposited $1,200—the entire payment for that year's crop. They kept only $5 for groceries. Later that day, the bank closed for good. Their $1,200 was gone, swallowed up along with their hopes and dreams.

New Yorkers lined up to withdraw their money.

People reacted in panic to the news of the crash.

GETTING THE NEWS

News of falling stock prices caused large crowds to gather near Wall Street. Without television or portable radios, news traveled much more slowly in 1929, so gathering on the street was a good way to get news firsthand.

HARD TIMES FOR KIT'S FAMILY

Like some, the Kittredges weren't directly affected when the stock market crashed in 1929. But by 1932, hard times hit Kit's family, too, when Mr. Kittredge had to close his car dealership because almost no one could afford a new car.

From the book Kit Learns a Lesson

Hardship and Hope

The stock market crash and its aftermath brought big changes to people and places across the country. Some of those changes created more hardship and suffering. Others brought progress and new hope to millions of Americans, and helped them hang on through the more than ten long years of the Depression.

① HOLLYWOOD!

In spite of hardships elsewhere, the movie industry was booming in the 1930s, and Hollywood became the movie capital of the world. Millions of Americans paid a hard-earned nickel or dime each week to see a movie that helped them forget their troubles for a while.

② DUST BOWL

During the 1930s, huge dust storms caused by not enough rain destroyed thousands of farms in the central part of the country—what came to be called the "Dust Bowl." Farmers actually helped create the Dust Bowl by overplanting the land and letting tons of rich topsoil blow away.

③ WORKER PROTESTS

During the 1930s, workers all across the nation started joining together to protest unsafe or unfair working conditions and to make sure that everyone had a fair chance for jobs. Workers' children often joined the protests.

④ ROUTE 66

Most who left Texas, Oklahoma, and the other Dust Bowl states for California traveled hopefully along Route 66, which they called the "Mother Road."

6 WALL STREET

New York City's Wall Street is a real street and is the home of the New York Stock Exchange and other financial institutions.

7 BENDIX AIR RACE

America's love affair with progress, speed, and daring was celebrated in the famous *Bendix Transcontinental Air Race*, a cross-country race between New York and Los Angeles. The first Bendix race was in 1931. Women competed, too, and made their mark in aviation with their first Bendix win in 1936. During this late-summer race, farmers all along the flight path eagerly watched the skies for a sight of some of the splendid Bendix racers.

8 NEW PRESIDENT—NEW HOPE

When President Hoover (left) didn't seem to do much to stop the Depression, Americans pinned their hopes instead on Franklin Delano Roosevelt (right). He won the 1932 election by a land-slide, moved to Washington, D.C., and started working on the nation's problems even *before* his March 1933 inauguration.

9

Because of new jobs programs created by Roosevelt, workers in the Civilian Conservation Corps (CCC) planted trees in Montana's Glacier National Park and in other parks across the country.

10 11

The Public Works Administration (PWA) sponsored dozens of public projects, including a port for Brownsville, Texas, and bridges connecting the island of Key West to Florida.

5 SKYSCRAPER!

Kit's hometown of Cincinnati escaped the first hard hit of the Depression, in part because of building projects started before the crash. The building of the magnificent 48-story Carew Tower, one of America's first skyscrapers, kept Cincinnatians employed and kept their hopes reaching skyward.

NOT ENOUGH

Americans were used to tough times, but the Depression was a different kind of tough time. For millions of Americans, the Great Depression meant not having enough—not enough work, or food, or clothes, or money. It meant doing without, making do, scraping by. For some people, it even meant losing their homes.

From the book Kit's Surprise

*Kit and Ruthie saw firsthand how some families were **evicted,** or thrown out of their homes, because they couldn't pay the rent.*

People wanted jobs, but there were not enough for everyone. Even employment agencies had few jobs to offer.

In 1930, the International Apple Shippers Association donated surplus apples for unemployed people to sell, but the apples soon ran out.

UNEMPLOYED
BUY APPLES
BUY APPLES 5c EACH

WANT AMID PLENTY

In 1931, the government's Farm Board had 250 million bushels of wheat stored—enough to bake millions of loaves of bread. But the government was afraid that giving out the wheat would make farm prices drop and make the Depression even worse. So the wheat rotted while families starved.

Children suffered when their parents didn't have enough money for shelter, food, or clothes.

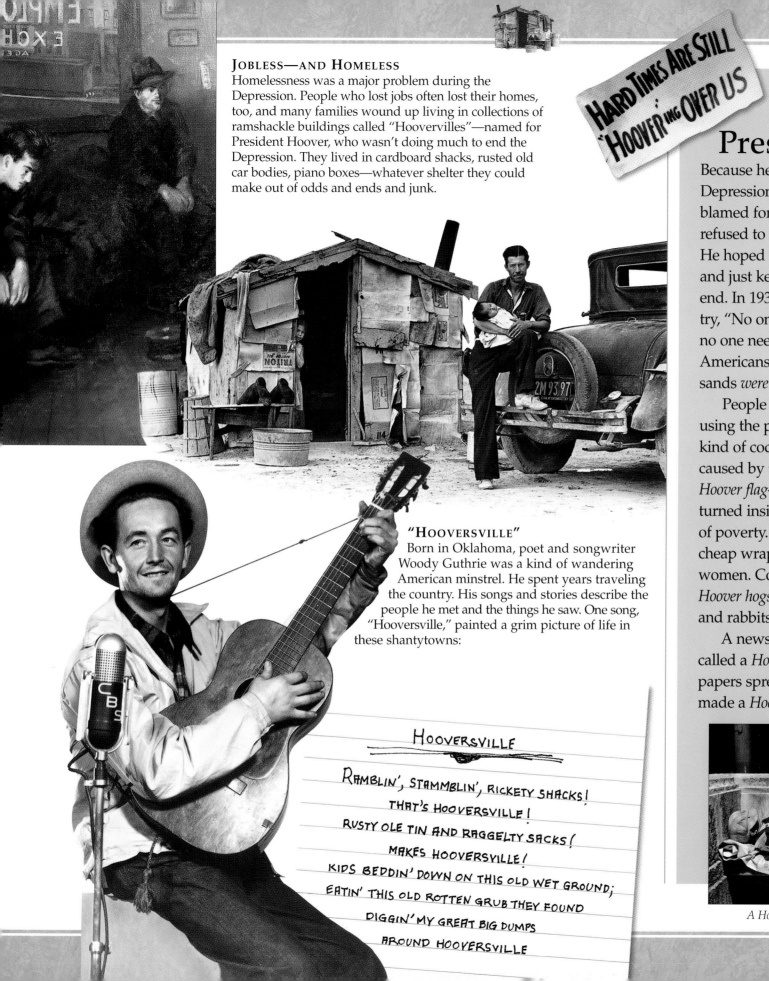

JOBLESS—AND HOMELESS

Homelessness was a major problem during the Depression. People who lost jobs often lost their homes, too, and many families wound up living in collections of ramshackle buildings called "Hoovervilles"—named for President Hoover, who wasn't doing much to end the Depression. They lived in cardboard shacks, rusted old car bodies, piano boxes—whatever shelter they could make out of odds and ends and junk.

"HOOVERSVILLE"

Born in Oklahoma, poet and songwriter Woody Guthrie was a kind of wandering American minstrel. He spent years traveling the country. His songs and stories describe the people he met and the things he saw. One song, "Hooversville," painted a grim picture of life in these shantytowns:

HOOVERSVILLE

RAMBLIN', STAMMBLIN', RICKETY SHACKS!
THAT'S HOOVERSVILLE!
RUSTY OLE TIN AND RAGGELTY SACKS!
MAKES HOOVERSVILLE!
KIDS BEDDIN' DOWN ON THIS OLD WET GROUND;
EATIN' THIS OLD ROTTEN GRUB THEY FOUND
DIGGIN' MY GREAT BIG DUMPS
AROUND HOOVERSVILLE

HARD TIMES ARE STILL "HOOVER ING OVER US

Blaming President Hoover

Because he was the president when the Depression started, Herbert Hoover was blamed for the nation's misery. Hoover refused to admit just how bad things were. He hoped that if Americans were cheerful and just kept going, the Depression would end. In 1931, for example, he told the country, "No one is going hungry, and no one need go hungry or cold." But Americans knew the truth—many thousands *were* hungry and cold that winter.

People showed their frustration by using the president's name as a kind of code for the troubles caused by the Depression. A *Hoover flag*—an empty pocket, turned inside out—was a sign of poverty. So were *Hoovers*, cheap wraparound dresses for women. Country people ate *Hoover hogs*—wild groundhogs and rabbits—to keep from starving.

A Hoover hog

A newspaper used as a blanket was called a *Hoover blanket*, and layers of newspapers spread on the ground or on a bench made a *Hoover mattress*.

A Hoover blanket and Hoover mattress

⊕ Hard Travelin'

After the stock market crash, thousands of Americans lost their homes and started to wander the country. They were known as *hoboes* or *tramps*—or, sometimes, *bums*. Many people were afraid of them and thought they were dangerous. More than half of these wanderers were teenagers or children. Most were boys or men, but there were hobo girls and women and even a few families. Hard times put most of these people on the road. Some teenagers left home so that their families would have one less mouth to feed. Others traveled the country looking for jobs. Some of them simply had nowhere else to go.

HOBO SONGS

Hoboes often passed the time singing about their travels. These are the words of a famous hobo song called "The Wabash Cannonball," which refers to the name of a train:

"Listen to the jingle, the rumble, and the roar,
As she glides along the woodlands,
By the hills and by the shore.
Hear the mighty rush of the engine,
Hear the lonesome hobo's call,
We're travelin' through the jungle
On the Wabash Cannonball."

HOBO CODE

Hoboes developed their own special language of symbols. They marked these symbols on houses, fences, and sidewalks to tell other wanderers what they might find.

FAMILIES ON THE ROAD

Many homeless families traveled by car, packing their belongings into or on top of their cars and leaving behind what they couldn't pack. Others traveled by foot or by train. Those who could afford a train ticket were lucky. Those who couldn't buy a ticket "rode the rails" instead.

Good Jungle

Hit the Road

Barking Dog

Beware— Danger

Kind Lady

Getting off a train could be risky, too, if a hobo ran into a **railroad bull**, or guard. Bulls sometimes used violence to make sure that hoboes kept moving once they got off a train.

RIDING THE RAILS

Hoboes and tramps traveled mostly by walking. But when they could, they *rode the rails*, hopping on trains without a ticket. Train travel was fast, but it was also scary. "Flipping a train," or jumping on while it was moving, was trickier—and more dangerous—than it looked.

Staying clean on the road was hard, and hoboes bathed and washed whenever they could. These hobo women traveled together for companionship and protection.

From the book Kit Saves the Day

Hoboes often stayed in hobo camps, called **jungles**, that were usually located close to a city's train station. When Kit and Stirling visited the jungle near Cincinnati's train station, they saw how hard hobo life was.

Almost all the places a hobo could ride—inside a boxcar, on the iron rods under a train car, or on top of a train car— were dangerous.

Courthouse or Judge

Bad Water

Someone with a Gun Nearby

Jail or Prison

Officer

GIRL HOBO

In 1932, the worst year of the Depression, Clydia Williams was seven years old. That was the year Clydia's mother got married and sent her away to live with relatives in Texas. The relatives didn't want Clydia, either. They left her alone for days at a time, along with her eight- and ten-year-old cousins, who were both boys.

When the boys began hopping freight trains, Clydia went with them. On the road, Clydia tied up her long hair and wore boys' clothes, because boy hoboes had more freedom than girls. A girl hobo could be kept by a mean-spirited housewife and made to work without pay. Besides, most of the other hobo kids were boys, so Clydia fit in better disguised as a boy.

If they had a choice, Clydia and her cousins rode in empty boxcars. Next best were cattle cars; they were noisy, because the frightened cows mooed and bellowed constantly, but otherwise safe. Hog cars were Clydia's least-favorite way to ride. The hogs were quieter than cattle, but they smelled terrible.

Clydia and her cousins did what they had to do to survive. They took food out of garbage cans and even swiped pies from porches. They shined shoes and did errands for cowboys. Sometimes storekeepers cheated them out of hard-earned money. Sometimes the poorest families shared the most with the hungry children.

For three years, Clydia spent months at a time on the road. The hobo life was hard, but she liked it. Riding the rails, she never felt unhappy, lonely, or unwanted. Lying in an empty boxcar with other tramps, the Oklahoma plains flying past, Clydia felt something new and wonderful: a sense of belonging and hope.

Hoboes and other train travelers who passed through Cincinnati in the early 1930s witnessed an amazing sight—a huge new train station under construction. In spite of bank failures and business closings in Cincinnati and across the country, the construction of the new terminal continued. That was good news for Cincinnati workers, because the building of Union Terminal provided hundreds of jobs. When completed in March of 1933, it was one of the most modern train stations in America. Some people even said that the station, designed in the new *Art Deco* style, looked like a giant radio!

① THE MAIN CONCOURSE
Huge murals showing Cincinnati's history greeted travelers entering the station through the main concourse. After buying train tickets, travelers could purchase newspapers and magazines, eat at any of several restaurants, browse in the toy shop, or visit the newsreel theater. They could even send telegrams from the station.

② THE NEWSREEL THEATER
Passengers waiting for trains could pass the time and stay informed watching newsreels in the terminal's theater. Each chair had a hat rack under the seat where men could store their hats while they watched.

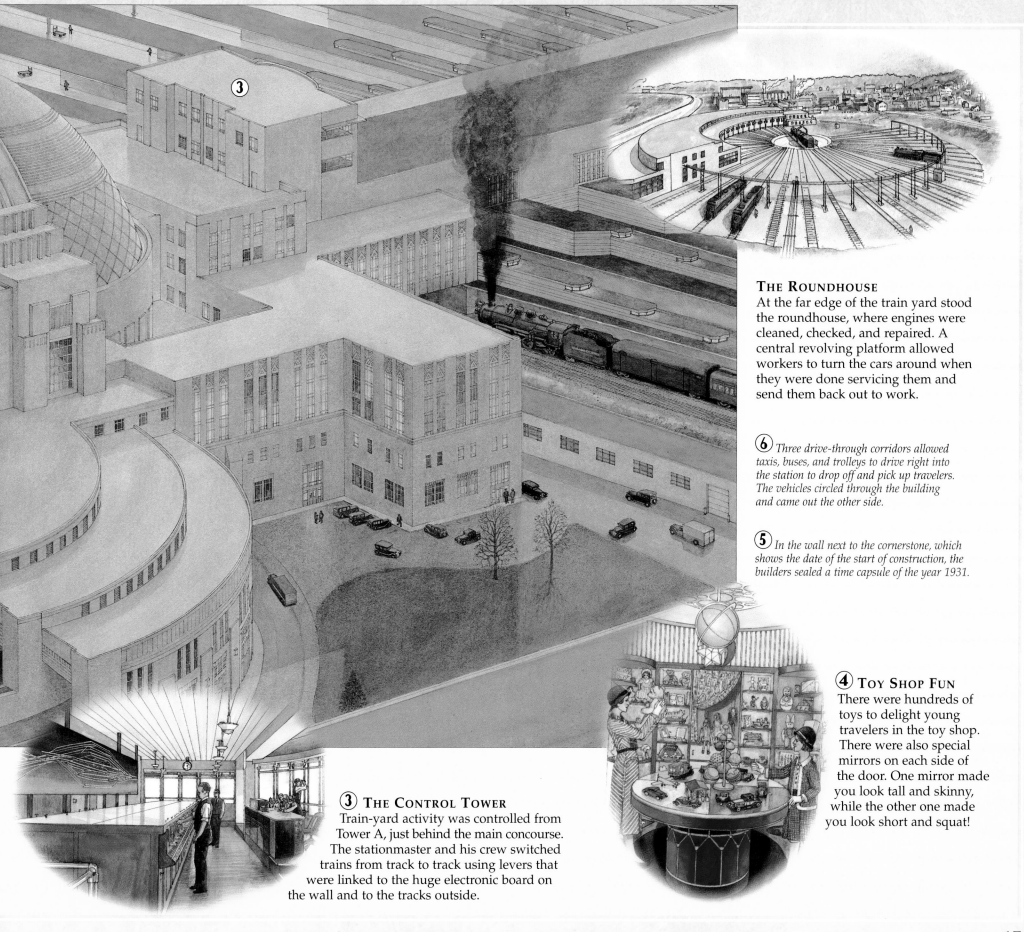

THE ROUNDHOUSE
At the far edge of the train yard stood the roundhouse, where engines were cleaned, checked, and repaired. A central revolving platform allowed workers to turn the cars around when they were done servicing them and send them back out to work.

⑥ *Three drive-through corridors allowed taxis, buses, and trolleys to drive right into the station to drop off and pick up travelers. The vehicles circled through the building and came out the other side.*

⑤ *In the wall next to the cornerstone, which shows the date of the start of construction, the builders sealed a time capsule of the year 1931.*

④ **TOY SHOP FUN**
There were hundreds of toys to delight young travelers in the toy shop. There were also special mirrors on each side of the door. One mirror made you look tall and skinny, while the other one made you look short and squat!

③ **THE CONTROL TOWER**
Train-yard activity was controlled from Tower A, just behind the main concourse. The stationmaster and his crew switched trains from track to track using levers that were linked to the huge electronic board on the wall and to the tracks outside.

In New York City, 82 soup kitchens served 85,000 meals a day.

The Winter of Despair

The winter of 1932–33 was a low point in American history. The Depression had been going on for three years, and for all anyone knew, it might go on forever. Many schools closed because there wasn't enough money to pay teachers. Businesses were closed because few people could afford their products or services. Men roamed the streets, desperate for work and food. Many Americans felt that the world they knew was dying, and the new world seemed to be a frightening and unfamiliar place.

BREAD LINES AND SOUP KITCHENS
Bread lines and soup kitchens saved many Americans from starving. Programs were usually run by churches or private charities and served a free meal of bread, soup, and coffee to anyone who showed up.

A NICE GUY?
Al Capone, a notorious gangster, ran a soup kitchen in Chicago to make himself more popular. Although he was a gangster, people were grateful for his help.

These children are waiting in line for milk.

DEPRESSION "MENUS"

Families like the Kittredges ate what they had to in order to survive. People gave these foods and meals names that made them sound more appetizing and colorful than they really were.

Instead of maple syrup, people poured "Depression syrup," made with water, sugar, and a drop of maple flavoring, over their pancakes.

Beans were called "miner's strawberries."

"Tomato soup" was ketchup and water.

People even earned money in flagpole-sitting contests!

DANCE TILL YOU DROP

People desperate for money participated in dance marathons. The last couple still on their feet won cash or prizes. Some marathons lasted for weeks, and partners took turns sleeping as they danced.

From the book Kit Learns a Lesson

Stale bread soaked in warm lard and water was called a "water sandwich." People sometimes poured "bulldog gravy"—flour, water, and a bit of grease—over their water sandwiches.

There were long lines of hungry people in Kit's hometown of Cincinnati, just as there were in cities all across the country.

17

Putting an End to Fear

The Americans who went to the polls in November 1932 were desperate for a change from the Hoover years. They elected an optimistic man named Franklin Delano Roosevelt, who was often referred to as "FDR." As governor of New York State, he had set up one of the first state-run relief organizations to help the unemployed during the Depression.

FDR pledged that, if elected, he would deliver "a new deal for the American people." He believed that his primary job as president was to rebuild hope throughout the nation. To do that, FDR brought in new people to help him put in place new policies and programs that he hoped would pull the country out of its severe economic and social slump.

Campaign buttons from the 1932 elections

A MAN OF ACTION
FDR was so active that most Americans did not realize that he was paralyzed from the waist down because of a disease called *polio*. He wore heavy metal braces on his legs and could not stand without canes or walk without help.

FRANKLIN AND ELEANOR
FDR's wife, Eleanor, campaigned by his side and acted as his "eyes and ears" in places that were hard for him to get to because he had difficulty walking.

FDR was a highly educated man from a privileged East Coast family, but wealthy and poor alike responded positively to his warmth and optimism.

FDR's campaign train, "The Roosevelt Special," took him across the country.

"THE ONLY THING WE HAVE TO FEAR IS FEAR ITSELF--"

Tickets to the 1933 presidential inauguration sold for $2—a lot of money during the Depression!

Mar. 4, 1933 THE NEW YORKER *Price 15 cents*

The unhappy outgoing President Hoover and the smiling new President Roosevelt rode together on the way to the inauguration.

FDR's INAUGURATION
Right from the start, President Roosevelt's words captured the hearts of the American people. In his inauguration speech on March 4, 1933, Roosevelt proclaimed, "The only thing we have to fear is fear itself." People believed FDR. And their belief and confidence helped bring about the end of the fearful times and a rebirth of hope.

A PRESIDENT ON THE RADIO
Franklin Roosevelt's inauguration speech was the first to be widely broadcast over the radio. His speech brought courage and hope to many Americans—and worried those who didn't like his politics.

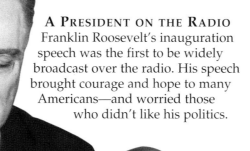

Spreading Fear
Germany experienced a serious depression at about the same time as America's Depression. Germans, too, chose a new leader who promised to solve their nation's problems. But Germany's leader, Adolf Hitler, became powerful in part by blaming Jewish people for Germany's hard times. By the late 1930s, this blame turned into violence against the Jews, who lost their political freedom, their businesses, and their homes. Hitler arrested and put Jews, and others he did not like, into prisons called *concentration camps*, where many died. Hitler also invaded other countries in Europe and arrested Jews everywhere he went. His actions led the world into another war: World War Two. Hitler *did* do what he'd promised—he pulled Germany out of its depression. But he did it at a terrible cost—the loss of millions of lives.

*Hitler's followers were called **Nazis**, and their symbol was a **swastika**. Once a symbol of good luck, it came to mean hatred.*

19

Weird Weather

Blowing topsoil quickly turned to dust and covered everything in its path.

All through the 1930s, weather across the country was extreme—frigid, snowy winters followed by sweltering summers. These weather patterns caused problems for farmers and made the effects of the Depression worse.

The worst year was 1936. In South Dakota that winter, the temperature was below zero for 35 days in a row, with blizzards every day for six weeks. In some parts of the state, no mail was delivered for more than a month, because letter carriers couldn't get through! That spring, heavy floods devastated New England. The summer that followed was unbearably hot and dry across the Great Plains. By May, the fields were brown and dry. One South Dakota man with hay fever recalls having no symptoms that year because there was no hay—or anything else—left growing.

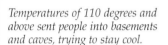

Temperatures of 110 degrees and above sent people into basements and caves, trying to stay cool.

Deep cracks in the earth formed when periods of extreme dryness were followed by heavy rains. On ground too hard to absorb it, rainwater washed away rich topsoil, forming gulleys and canyons where crops used to grow.

DUST BOWL DINNER

When 10-year-old Lila Williams set the dinner table, everything—plates, glasses, and coffee cups—went upside down. When the plates and cups were turned over, they were clean, even when the rest of the table was covered with fine sand. Dust and sand got into all the food, of course. Lila's father made jokes about not having to pepper the potatoes, and he teased Lila about drinking "chocolate" milk!

PRAYING FOR RAIN

During one long drought in 1931, people in a small South Dakota town took out a newspaper ad that read, "Wanted: Rain . . . must be delivered soon to do any good." In 1934, traveling salesmen carried machines that were supposed to help make rain. That same year, "prayer bands" popped up all over Kansas—groups of people who prayed together for rain. Unfortunately, none of it helped, and the drought continued.

Pumping water was especially hard during a dust storm. People had to cover their mouths and noses to keep the dust out.

Farm Strikes

During the Depression, crop prices dropped so low that it often cost farmers more to grow crops than they could earn by selling them. In 1932, for instance, a bushel of corn sold for 22¢—but raising that corn cost a farmer close to 90¢.

Farmers got mad—and they decided to do something about it. In August 1932 they organized a "Farmers' Holiday," a whole month when farmers went on strike and refused to sell any crops at all. They hoped their strike would raise prices and make people pay attention to the problems farmers were having.

They *did* attract attention. But people were upset to read about groups of farmers blocking shipments of milk and produce, or worse—dumping out or destroying food to keep it from reaching stores. Later in the year, desperate farmers marched on Washington, D.C., demanding help from the government. But help did not come until long afterward, and many farmers lost their farms and homes before it arrived.

This farmer is protesting by pouring out cream that was trucked in from another state to break the farm strike.

21

Black Blizzard

The dust storms of the 1930s were terrifying events that lasted for hours and sometimes days at a time. Dust got into everything—food, houses, machines. People blew their noses and mud came out. Animals suffocated from breathing too much dust. People got lost just yards from their own front door.

One of the worst "black blizzards" rolled through the Great Plains on April 14, 1935—a day later known as Black Sunday. For the rest of their lives, people remembered where they had been and what they had been doing on Black Sunday.

Voices from the Dust Bowl

"It was eerie to look across the countryside and see curtains of thick sand blowing, with thousands of tumbling weeds rolling ahead of the dust, spinning on and on until they were caught by the fence rows. . . . There were times it became dark as night in the afternoon, and chickens went to roost. . . . There were times we could write our names in the sand on our table. A slow lick of the lips would give us a taste of mud."

LEE NELSON, TEXAS

"We kept the doors and windows all shut tight, with wet papers on the sills. The tiny particles of dirt sifted right through the walls. . . . Our faces looked like coal miners', our hair was gray and stiff with dirt, and we ground dirt in our teeth. . . . Sometimes there was a fog all through the house and all we could do about it was sit on our dusty chairs and see that fog settle slowly and silently over everything."

GRACE TEMPLIN STOLSON, KANSAS

"We had to brace ourselves against the wind. Oh, how the sand stung our legs, hands, and whatever part of our face that showed. . . . Lots of times we walked backward to school."

BONNIE REID, OKLAHOMA

I arise in the morning,
greet the world with a grin,
Ten minutes later,
I'm in dirt to my chin;
I grab up the broom,
I grab up the mop,
I start in cleaning and never stop;
I don't dare stop,
'cause if I do,
Sure as heck,
we couldn't wade thru.

DUST EVERYWHERE
The dust storms made everyday life a challenge. Keeping things clean was a full-time job. One Kansas woman wrote this funny poem about it.

Floods . . . and Grasshoppers

While dry spells and dust storms devastated the Great Plains, flooding was a major problem in other parts of the country. In 1937, Kit's hometown of Cincinnati had the worst flood of its history when the Ohio River rose more than 37 feet and flooded the whole city. People who had started to recover from the early years of the Depression faced yet another crisis when they lost their homes, businesses, and jobs to the flood. Another devastation came in the form of grasshoppers. In the dry years of the 1930s, grasshoppers hatched by the millions and ate their way through the entire countryside. Swarming clouds of grasshoppers would arrive and devour everything in sight before moving on. One Nebraska farm girl accidentally left her favorite doll outside overnight—and the grasshoppers ate the clothes right off its body!

Coney Island, Cincinnati, Ohio

ROLLER COASTER
The Ohio River flood of 1937 was the worst flood Cincinnati and Kentucky had ever seen. Coney Island Amusement Park, located on an island in the Ohio River, was underwater for weeks and was nearly destroyed.

A Fruitless Battle

Margaret and Dorothy could hardly believe it: their family's newly rented North Dakota farm had two apple trees! All spring the sisters watched the pink and white flowers turn to tiny apples, and they dreamed of eating apple dumplings, apple pie, and other rare treats.

Then one terrible afternoon, a dark cloud settled on the farm—millions of newly hatched grasshoppers. The pests ate the family's whole crop of grain. When they moved on to the apple trees, the girls were determined to stop them. Margaret set a large washtub under one tree and filled it with water. Then she and Dorothy climbed the tree and began knocking grasshoppers into the tub, where they drowned.

But no matter how many hungry grasshoppers the girls killed, more came to take their places. Margaret cried as she watched the grasshoppers eat the leaves and the bite-sized apples. The insects left behind only apple cores, dangling from bare branches, and two girls who would never forget the misery they had caused.

Some farmers gave up battling grasshoppers and left for land farther west.

OREGON OR BUST

Okies

In cars packed with everything they had, Midwesterners went west in search of a better life.

When their cars broke down, people had to walk their way west.

Faced with disaster after disaster, many Great Plains farmers just gave up. They packed their belongings into beat-up cars or trucks or on their backs, gathered their families, and left the cracked and dusty land. Like the pioneers 100 years before, they went west, toward the place they'd heard was rich and welcoming: California.

But California, too, had its share of misery. There was plenty of work—picking cotton and peaches and other crops—but it didn't pay much, and there wasn't enough to support the streams of poor travelers from the east. People in California were afraid that the new arrivals—known as "Okies," because so many were from Oklahoma—would make their own lives harder. Okies were considered to be poor, lazy, and dirty. Most of all, they were unwanted.

Instead of going to school, many children worked in the fields alongside their parents. This girl had to fill her long sack with the cotton she picked.

THE FACE OF HARDSHIP
The families who reached California without money or decent jobs faced many difficulties. Just keeping clean was a challenge. Sometimes the only place to wash up was in an irrigation ditch.

26

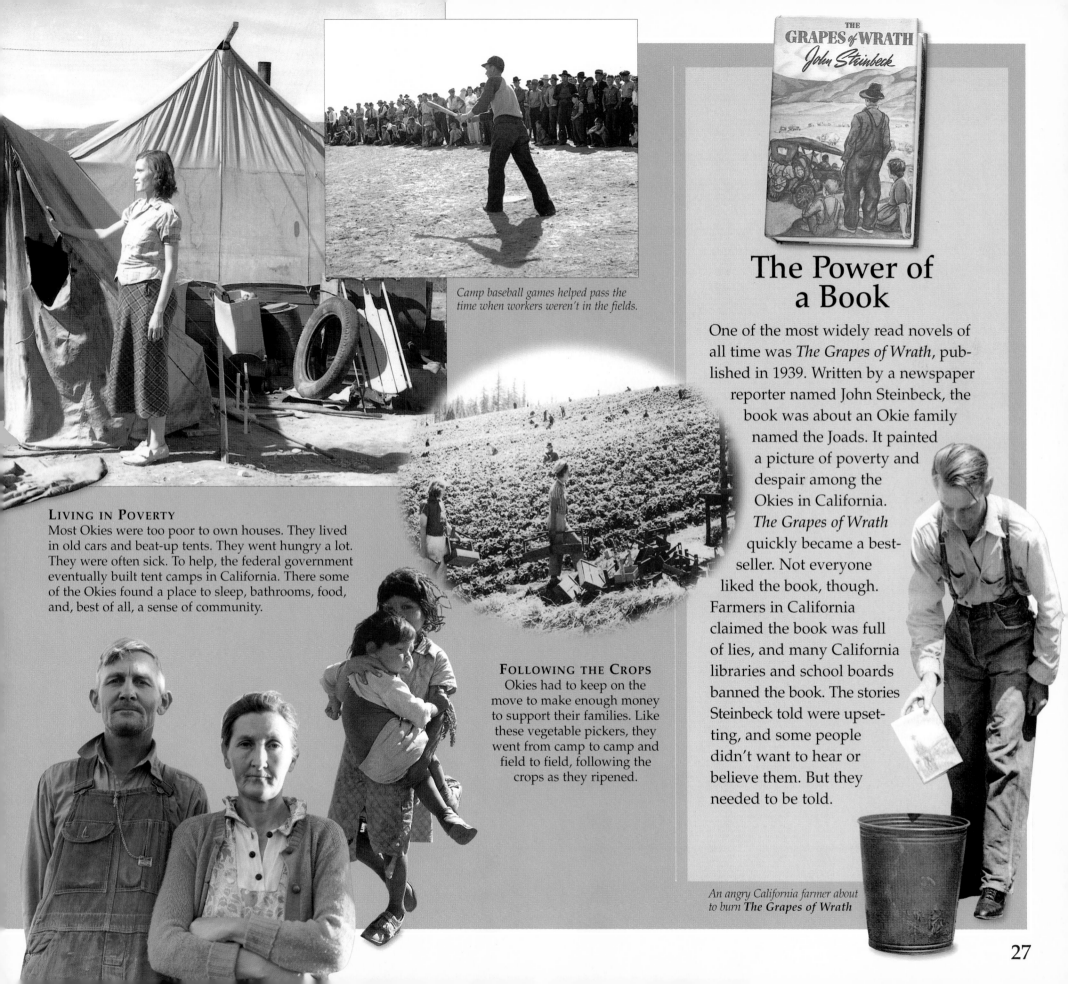

Camp baseball games helped pass the time when workers weren't in the fields.

The Power of a Book

One of the most widely read novels of all time was *The Grapes of Wrath*, published in 1939. Written by a newspaper reporter named John Steinbeck, the book was about an Okie family named the Joads. It painted a picture of poverty and despair among the Okies in California. *The Grapes of Wrath* quickly became a bestseller. Not everyone liked the book, though. Farmers in California claimed the book was full of lies, and many California libraries and school boards banned the book. The stories Steinbeck told were upsetting, and some people didn't want to hear or believe them. But they needed to be told.

LIVING IN POVERTY

Most Okies were too poor to own houses. They lived in old cars and beat-up tents. They went hungry a lot. They were often sick. To help, the federal government eventually built tent camps in California. There some of the Okies found a place to sleep, bathrooms, food, and, best of all, a sense of community.

FOLLOWING THE CROPS

Okies had to keep on the move to make enough money to support their families. Like these vegetable pickers, they went from camp to camp and field to field, following the crops as they ripened.

An angry California farmer about to burn *The Grapes of Wrath*

A Depression for All

Many African Americans were already poor when the Depression began. Years of discrimination had kept them from good jobs, good schools, and a better life. For them, the 1930s brought more of the same hardships they already faced. As one black man said, the Depression "only became official when it happened to the white man."

The Depression did not discriminate, but the U.S. government did. In Atlanta, Georgia, the average monthly relief check for a white person was $32.66. Blacks received only $19.29, because the government decided they needed less. Even new jobs programs designed to fight the Depression provided more and better jobs for white men and women than for black men and women, or for Native Americans.

FEW GOOD JOBS
Because of *prejudice*, or unreasonable dislike of individuals or groups of people, blacks had fewer job choices than white people did. Most blacks could get only low-paying jobs that white people did not want.

IN THE COUNTRY
In the rural South, many black people worked as *sharecroppers*. They raised crops on land owned by someone else—usually white landowners. Sharecroppers gave part of their crops to the landowners and sold the rest. But some landowners cheated sharecroppers, which helped keep them in poverty.

Some sharecropping families couldn't afford anything more than a rough shack.

SEGREGATION
Most states had laws to *segregate,* or separate, black people from white people. Black people had to use separate bathrooms, barbers, entrances to public buildings, and even phone booths. They also used separate areas in restaurants and hotels and on buses and trains.

IN THE CITY
Life for black people wasn't much better in the city. Prejudice and segregation often forced blacks to live in areas that were crowded and dirty.

Public swimming classes paid for by the government were segregated, too, mainly because the pools in which the classes were taught were segregated.

SEPARATE AND VERY UNEQUAL
In many areas, African American children were taught at home or went to all-black schools. The courts had said that such schools could be "separate" but had to be "equal" to the schools for white children, but they seldom were.

THREATS OF VIOLENCE
In the 1930s, racial prejudice sometimes led to violence, and many black people lived with the threat of violence shadowing their lives. Mobs of whites sometimes went after blacks for supposed crimes and killed them, often by hanging.

ON THE RESERVATION
Native Americans struggled with grinding poverty, made worse by the Depression. To earn $10 to feed her family, one woman finally sold the last thing of value she had—her grandmother's elegantly beaded ceremonial dress, which she never saw again.

America's Other Voices

Poet Langston Hughes became famous during the 1920s in an important literary movement known as the Harlem Renaissance. His poem, "I, Too," voiced the need of black people to be recognized as part of the fabric of American life.

I, too, sing America.

*I am the darker brother.
They send me to eat in the kitchen
When company comes;
But I laugh,
And eat well,
And grow strong.*

*Tomorrow,
I'll be at the table
When company comes.
Nobody'll dare
Say to me,
"Eat in the kitchen,"
Then.*

*Besides,
They'll see how beautiful I am
And be ashamed—*

I, too, am America.

"We Didn't Know We Were Poor"

The Depression touched just about every American family. But children sometimes didn't realize just how hard times were for their own families. Almost everyone they knew was poor, so they didn't think of themselves as being deprived or different. Years later, when they had grown up, many of those kids said the same thing about their childhoods: "We didn't know we were poor."

Children often didn't feel ashamed to wear hand-me-down clothing because everyone else was wearing it, too!

New York City used its water system to create sprinklers so that kids could keep cool during hot weather.

A NEW GAME

In 1935, *Monopoly*, a new game that let you pretend you were wealthy enough to buy and sell property, was the best-selling game in America. The unemployed creator of the game, Charles Darrow, became a millionaire!

A skate key was needed to tighten the clamps that held the front of the skate to the shoe.

FUN ON WHEELS

Roller-skating was a fun, no-cost activity for children whose families had roller skates. Kids strapped their skates onto their shoes and skated for free in parks and on city streets and sidewalks.

TOYS ON LOAN

One of President Roosevelt's new government programs was a toy-lending program. It worked much like a library—but instead of books, children could borrow a different toy every few weeks.

This girl picked out a miniature electric stove that really worked.

A RACE TO THE FINISH

Stilts were cheap and easy to make from scraps of leftover wood, and stilt-racing was great fun.

SURPRISE!

People came up with creative ways to help one another survive. In one town, neighbors held "surprise parties." They would knock on a family's door in the evening and surprise them with a party. They'd present the family with gifts of food and money. The gifts helped—and so did the love and caring that came along with them.

The Secret Helpers Club

Like girls all over the country, 12-year-old Toni Johnson and her friends wanted to prove they could help, too. So they started a club called the Secret Helpers. Dues were 10¢ a week, which the girls used to buy soup and bread. Every week Toni and her friends filled a box with the food they'd bought and left it on the porch of a poor family in their small town in Maine. They rang the doorbell and ran away, so no one knew who left the food. Sometimes they left shoes, mittens, and money with the food. Toni loved being part of the Secret Helpers Club.

Making D

People made do in all kinds of ways during the Depression. They dreamed up ways to make their own clothes, their own meals, their own fun—even their own schools! People recycled almost everything in the 1930s—long before the word *recycle* was ever used. Sometimes there didn't seem to be enough to go around, but they figured out new ways to stretch just one more use out of everything they had.

Children like Kit helped their families by working in their vegetable gardens.

MAKING PRESERVES

Home gardeners got serious during the Depression. Families turned their flower beds into gardens that provided fresh food during the summer and preserves to last through the winter.

MAKING IT LAST

The girl on the right (above) was given a hand-me-down coat when she was two—and she wore it for eight years!

MAKING MUSIC

Family sing-alongs and neighborhood concerts made for no-cost, do-it-yourself fun.

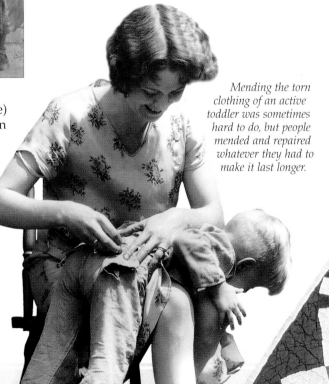

Mending the torn clothing of an active toddler was sometimes hard to do, but people mended and repaired whatever they had to make it last longer.

MAKING MONEY

When businesses and government agencies ran out of money during the Depression, some created IOUs and special coupons called *scrip*, which could be used as money. IOUs were sometimes as simple as a dollar amount written on a clam shell!

MAKING QUILTS

There was a return to quilting during the 1930s, as families on tight budgets found one more use for their old clothes. Quilting turned scraps into a treasure that was both practical and beautiful.

Weedpatch School

The people who lived in the Arvin Federal Camp, one of the government's Okie camps in California, had their own name for the dusty, rocky camp: Weedpatch Camp. For the children who lived there, the worst part of life at the camp was having to leave it every morning to go to the local school. Some had never been to school before. Many could not read or write. At school, the other kids teased and humiliated them. Teachers treated them as if they were stupid.

Luckily, one man believed in them: the Kern County school superintendent, Mr. Leo Hart. Mr. Hart visited Weedpatch Camp every week. He played ball with the children and talked to them. He understood that they were, as he said, "ordinary kids, with the same hopes and dreams the rest of us have."

When local parents and school officials demanded that the Weedpatch children be kicked out of "their" public schools, Mr. Hart decided it was time for the Okie kids to have a school of their own. So one September morning, he and the children began building their school. They did everything themselves, from putting up outhouses to laying pipes to building desks and chairs. They planted potatoes and raised their own pigs. They learned to read, to type, to cook, to swim. They used donated and leftover materials and turned them into

a wonderful treasure. The school was so successful that "regular" parents began trying to get their kids into the Okie school!

But the most important lesson taught at the school wasn't in the curriculum. Thanks to Mr. Hart—and wonderful teachers—the 400 students of Weedpatch School learned to be proud of themselves and who they were. And that was a lesson that stayed with them for the rest of their lives.

Boarding House

Many families did what Kit's family did when jobs were lost and money was scarce—they took in boarders in order to keep their house and pay their *mortgage*, the amount owed to the bank for a home loan. Boarders paid by the week or month for a room and meals with the family. Homes became crowded as extended-family members and boarders moved in. Bedrooms, attics, and even living rooms were shared or divided to make room for everyone.

AN EXTRA BEDROOM
A sunporch could easily become an extra bedroom.

THE FAMILY CAR
Families lucky enough to keep their cars took good care of them so they'd last a long time. Some people could afford gasoline, but few could afford to buy new cars.

Money for home repairs was hard to come by, so peeling paint or missing shingles sometimes didn't get fixed right away.

Women often did other people's laundry and ironing to earn extra money. They also saved money by knitting and sewing clothes for the whole family.

Children made scooters out of scrap wood, "tommy-walkers" for their feet out of tin cans and string, and jump ropes from spare rope.

(1) *Storage was often a problem when extra people moved in. Families added pegs on walls, used storage chests, and even stored things in boxes under beds and dressers.*

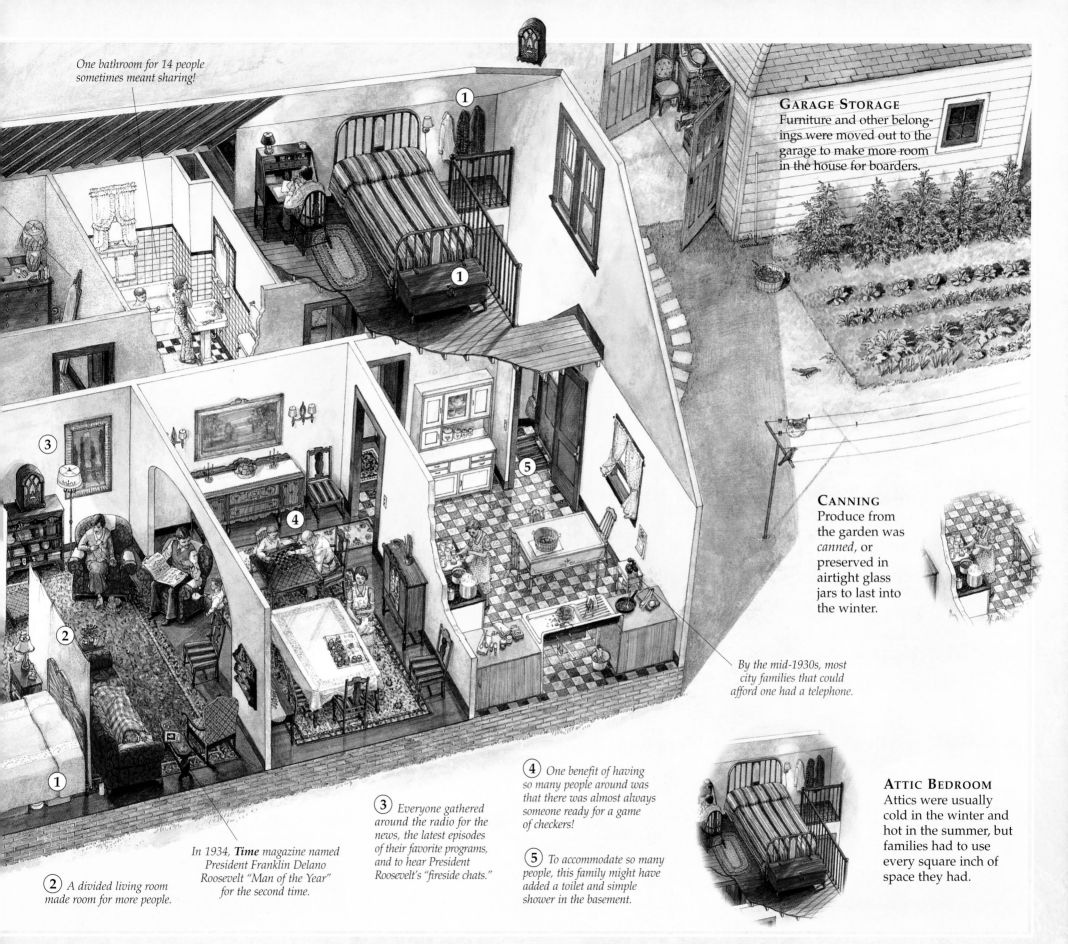

One bathroom for 14 people sometimes meant sharing!

GARAGE STORAGE
Furniture and other belongings were moved out to the garage to make more room in the house for boarders.

CANNING
Produce from the garden was *canned*, or preserved in airtight glass jars to last into the winter.

By the mid-1930s, most city families that could afford one had a telephone.

ATTIC BEDROOM
Attics were usually cold in the winter and hot in the summer, but families had to use every square inch of space they had.

③ In 1934, **Time** magazine named President Franklin Delano Roosevelt "Man of the Year" for the second time.

② A divided living room made room for more people.

③ Everyone gathered around the radio for the news, the latest episodes of their favorite programs, and to hear President Roosevelt's "fireside chats."

④ One benefit of having so many people around was that there was almost always someone ready for a game of checkers!

⑤ To accommodate so many people, this family might have added a toilet and simple shower in the basement.

The Gift of a Lifetime

Life was never easy in the tiny mountain community of Shady Cove, but especially not during the Depression. Children went barefoot and hungry. They had no toys or dolls. The schoolteacher, Miss Enslow, tried to help. She made dolls out of tin cans and bottles decorated with scraps of fabric, and she wished she could do more for each child she taught.

One spring day in 1934, Miss Enslow got her chance to help one of them. That day, seven-year-old Amelia Cavin was helping her family cut firewood. Amelia reached for a block of wood just as her brother brought down an ax.

Miss Enslow rushed to the Cavins' home as soon as she heard about the accident. She arrived at the same time as the doctor. Amelia's dress was soaked with blood, and Amelia was so terrified that she wouldn't let the doctor near her.

Miss Enslow knelt beside Amelia. She said that if Amelia would let the doctor take care of her hand, she would buy the girl something she really wanted.

"I'd like to have a doll!" sobbed Amelia.

"You shall have it," promised the teacher.

The doctor had begun examining Amelia's hand when she whispered, "Miss Enslow, can the doll have red hair?"

"If they make them with red hair," said the teacher, "you shall have one."

The teacher drove 40 miles to the nearest city. In store after store she saw dolls with dark curls and blond ringlets, but not one had red hair. Finally, as the last store was about to close, a clerk found a single red-haired doll in a basement stockroom.

The doll cost $5.98. Miss Enslow thought about what that money could buy for the hungry children of Shady Cove: 200 pounds of flour, 22 quarts of peanut butter, 177 loaves of bread, or 39 pounds of ground meat. But she had made a promise she knew she had to keep.

Hours later, she walked up the narrow, mile-long trail to the Cavins' cabin. It was late at night, but the whole family was awake and waiting. The teacher laid a large box in front of the fire and took off the lid so that the firelight gleamed on the doll inside.

"Oh, look," whispered Amelia, "it's got red hair!"

Miss Enslow couldn't mend Amelia's hand or take away her pain, but she could show Amelia how important she was, and that her worth wasn't measured by how wealthy she was. Miss Enslow gave her love, courage, self-respect, and hope—priceless gifts that would last a lifetime.

Outdoor Fun

Most outdoor fun didn't cost anything. Kids could run through sprinklers, jump rope, play hopscotch and baseball, and fly homemade kites without spending any money. One girl growing up in New York City took long walks through the city with her unemployed dad. They also played card games and checkers on the steps of their apartment building while they listened to the radio through an open window. She loved their time outdoors together and she loved having her dad at home—even though she knew it was hard for him not to have a job.

KEEPING COOL
During the hot summers of the 1930s, kids cooled down by running through their sprinklers.

The first drive-in movie theater was built in New Jersey in 1939. For $1, a whole family could crowd into the car and forget about their troubles for an hour or two.

GO FLY A KITE!
Even families without much money had the makings of a kite: sticks, paper, string, and colorful rags for the kite's tail.

DRIVE-IN THEATRE
"WORLD'S FIRST"
SIT IN YOUR CAR
SEE AND HEAR
MOVIES
25¢   25¢
PER CAR   PER PERSON
3 OR MORE PERSONS ONE DOLLAR
OPEN TO-NIGHT

BATTER UP!
Kids played "kitten ball" or "mushball" on city streets and playgrounds. These early versions of softball used a large, mushy ball instead of the small, hard one used in baseball.

CINCINNATI REDS

MIDGET GOLF
Miniature golf was created during the Depression and was called "midget golf." A small course with a series of makeshift obstacles could easily be set up on an empty lot.

"THE SCHNOZZ"
Some popular baseball players had colorful nicknames, like "The Babe," "Lefty," or "Dizzy." Cincinnati Reds catcher Ernie Lombardi was affectionately known as "The Schnozz" because of his large nose!

A BASEBALL FIRST
The first night game by a professional baseball team was played in Kit's hometown of Cincinnati in 1935—and President Roosevelt turned on the field lights from the White House! Night games provided a weekday opportunity for working fans to attend a game, which increased ticket sales and helped keep the Reds in business.

Rich in Imaginati☉n

Many people turned to the world of reading to escape the hard times. Library books were free, inexpensive comic books of all kinds were available, and comic strips were printed in the newspaper. Many of the same characters turned up in the comics *and* on the radio, so you could follow their adventures in two ways.

Millions of Americans tuned in to popular radio shows each night. Sitting beside the radio, they could forget their troubles for a little while and lose themselves in the world of imagination.

A good friend, a good book, and the perfect reading spot made for hours of enjoyment.

Buck Rogers *was a series of science fiction stories that was much loved by anyone who liked a good adventure story.*

NOT JUST FOR KIDS
Little Orphan Annie and her trusty dog, Sandy, got into and out of all sorts of jams—but they always triumphed in the end. Annie's adventures delighted children and adults alike.

Orphan Annie fans could help Annie solve mysteries by sending for and using this special Orphan Annie Decoder Badge!

RADIO STYLES
Radios became sleeker and smaller as radio technology improved during the 1930s. Instead of looming large in the middle of the living room, the new smaller radios could sit on kitchen counters or bedside tables.

Rin-Tin-Tin barks into a microphone to warn of danger!

REGULARLY SCHEDULED PROGRAMS
People planned their schedules so that they wouldn't miss a single episode of their favorite shows. Here's a newspaper listing of the radio shows Kit and other Cincinnati listeners could have heard on a typical Thursday.

9:00 KSD—MAREK WE TRA.

Drama and Sketches

5:00 KWK—Don Winslow of the Navy.
5:15 KSD—DICK TRACY.
  KMOX—Howie Wing.
5:30 KWK—Terry and the Pirates.
5:45 KSD—CAPTAIN MIDNIGHT.
  KMOX—Little Orphan Annie. KWK
  —Tom Mix, Straight Shooters.
6:00 KSD—AMOS AND ANDY.
  KWK—Alias Jimmy Valentine.
6:15 KMOX—Lum and Abner.
6:30 KSD—"CAPTAINS IN PERIL."
7:30 KWK—Those We Love.
8:00 KMOX—Radio Theater; Carole Lombard, Basil Rathbone and Jeffrey Lynn.
9:30 KSD — DETECTIVE MYSTERY STORIES.
10:00 KMOX—The Goldbergs.

6:30
7:40
8:45
8:35
10:

Dance Music Tonight

War of the Worlds

Newspapers around the country reported news of the broadcast.

On the night before Halloween in 1938, families listening to their radios got the shock of their lives. A news flash reported that martians had invaded Earth! The announcer described strange flying machines and little green aliens. Millions of people panicked and called police stations. Families prayed and cried, convinced they were about to die.

Was there a martian invasion? Of course not! What radio listeners were hearing was actually a play called "The War of the Worlds," the creation of a young actor named Orson Welles. The fact that the play terrified so many people demonstrated just how powerful radio had become in the lives of most Americans.

Orson Welles at work in the CBS radio studio

At the Movies

Eighty million people went to the movies every week—more than half the population of America! Sitting in front of the big silver screen, they lost themselves in the imaginary worlds that filled the screen. Glamorous dancing girls, dangerous gangsters, goofy comedians, and an adorable young actress named Shirley Temple provided a welcome escape from the often-harsh daily realities of the Depression.

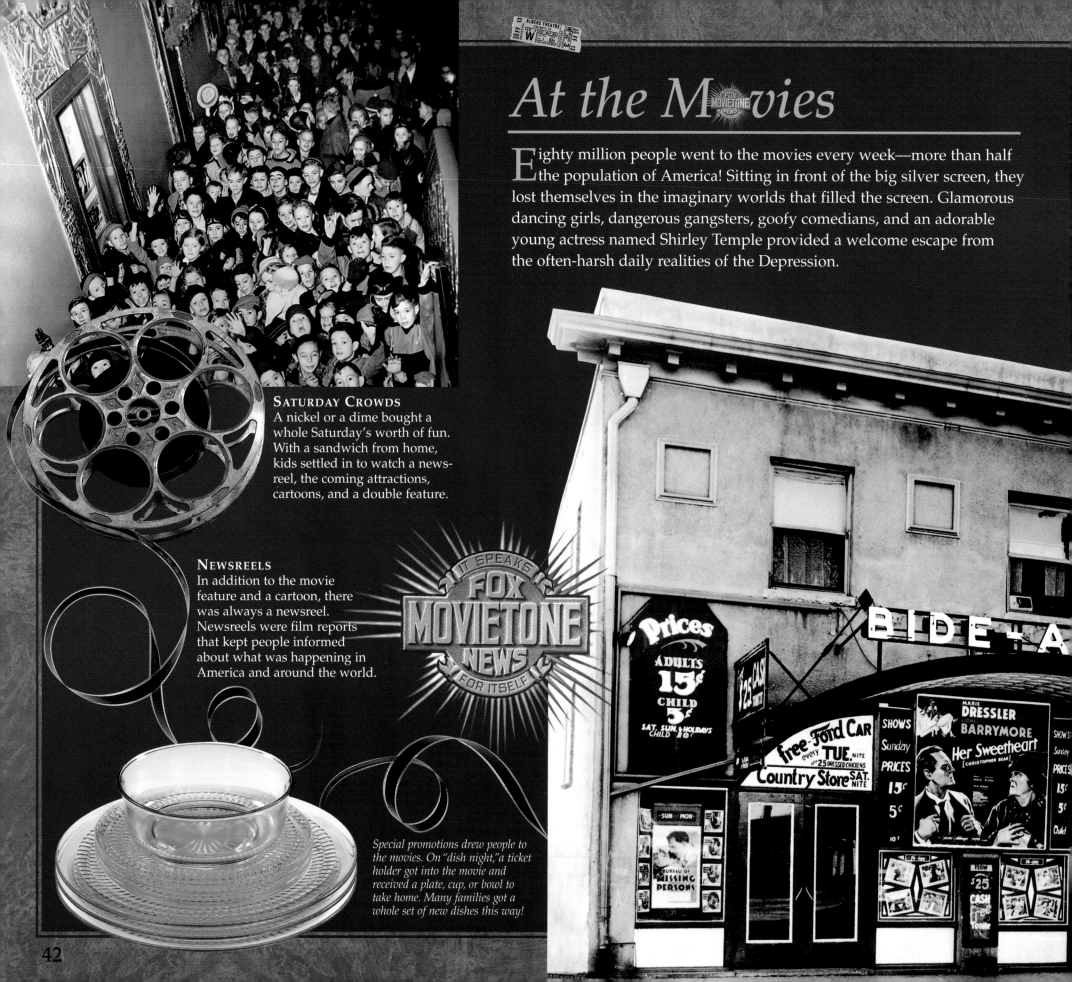

SATURDAY CROWDS
A nickel or a dime bought a whole Saturday's worth of fun. With a sandwich from home, kids settled in to watch a newsreel, the coming attractions, cartoons, and a double feature.

NEWSREELS
In addition to the movie feature and a cartoon, there was always a newsreel. Newsreels were film reports that kept people informed about what was happening in America and around the world.

Special promotions drew people to the movies. On "dish night," a ticket holder got into the movie and received a plate, cup, or bowl to take home. Many families got a whole set of new dishes this way!

DANCING DWARFS
Feature-length cartoons like Disney's *Snow White and the Seven Dwarfs* delighted and distracted audiences of all ages.

Shirley Temple starred in Rebecca of Sunnybrook Farm, a 1939 black-and-white movie. Color film was new but expensive, so most movies were still made with black-and-white film.

MUSICAL EXTRAVAGANZAS
The extravagant musicals of the 1930s featured elaborate stage sets, fancy costumes, complicated choreography, and extraordinary props. White violins trimmed with white neon provided a special glow to the dancing girls in the movie *Gold Diggers of 1933*.

A neon-trimmed movie prop

A NEW REALISM
When *Gone With the Wind* opened in 1939, people were shocked that it cost so much—a whole 75¢! Of course, the movie did last almost four hours! Advances in movie-making technology brought a new feeling of realism. Some people in the audience said they could feel the heat from the flames in the scene where Atlanta burned!

AMERICA'S SWEETHEART
Young Shirley Temple captured the hearts of Americans of all ages when she first appeared in the movies at age three. Americans liked her spunky optimism and sweet face.

A ticket to an early showing of Gone With the Wind—83¢ with tax!

*People took heart when Judy Garland, the 16-year-old star of **The Wizard of Oz**, sang of finding hope "somewhere over the rainbow."*

Heroines in the Sky

In 1932, Amelia Earhart became the first woman to fly solo across the Atlantic Ocean. Newspapers and movie newsreels were filled with the details of her flight, and her accomplishment thrilled people everywhere. Girls like Kit dreamed of daring deeds, just like Amelia's.

Women all over the country took to the air in the 1920s and 1930s. They flew every kind of plane and worked as test pilots, crop dusters, mail carriers, and stunt fliers. On their way to becoming pilots, most had to overcome the disapproval of those who thought women couldn't—or shouldn't—be pilots. But each was determined to do what she loved best—to fly.

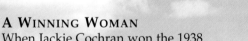

You are Invited to Attend
ARRASMITH FIELD DEDICATION & AIR SHOW
TUESDAY and WEDNESDAY, SEPT. 28-29

MISS EVELYN SHARP
America's Youngest Licensed Pilot of Ord, Nebr.,
will be in Our Store on these Two Days to Meet
Her Many Admirers and Give Autographs

Evelyn Sharp

Present This Card for Autographing in Above Space

"I Want to Drive an Airplane"
At age nine, Evelyn Sharp told a friend, "I want to drive an airplane." As an adult, she did just that, often flying her beloved Curtiss Robin monoplane with her dog, Scottie, in a seat behind her. "Sharpie," as she was called, never let anything stop her, including a lifelong struggle with asthma.

This ticket and airplane were part of a promotion to celebrate the opening of a Nebraska airfield. Evelyn Sharp was the first pilot to land at the new field.

Many early pilots carried mailbags for the U.S. Post Office in the first days of airmail service.

A Winning Woman
When Jackie Cochran won the 1938 Bendix Race, the most famous air race in America, her victory led to a rumor that a man had secretly flown her plane for her!

First Lady Eleanor Roosevelt, who loved to fly, presented Jackie Cochran (on the left) with one of the three Harmon Trophies Cochran won for being the outstanding woman flier in the world.

Parachute pack

Extra cushions were sometimes needed for height because planes weren't designed with women in mind.

Amelia Earhart flew a Lockheed Vega airplane like this one on her 1932 solo flight across the Atlantic.

"I Like to Fly ... and I'm Restless"

Amelia Earhart and her plane disappeared over the Pacific Ocean on a round-the-world flight in July 1937. "Women must try to do things as men have tried," she wrote just before her last flight. "When they fail, their failure must be but a challenge to others."

An aviator cap and goggles were a must for pilots—some early planes didn't have glass in the window openings!

Saved by a Parachute

In 1930, stunt pilot Mildred Kaufman, at left, became a member of the *Caterpillar Club*. This club, which was established in 1922, had very special members—pilots whose lives were saved by their parachutes. The name was selected because caterpillars spin the silk that is used for parachute sails and lines, and a caterpillar must emerge from its cocoon in order to survive—just like the pilots who had to jump from their planes.

Club members received pins like this.

Another First

Anne Morrow Lindbergh was the first American woman to earn a first-class glider pilot's license, in 1930. She and her pilot husband, Charles "Lucky" Lindbergh, were a famous husband-and-wife flying team.

Packing Light

Planes couldn't carry any extra weight, so a pilot was limited to carrying just a few items. When Amelia Earhart made her historic solo flight across the Atlantic Ocean in 1932, she carried little besides maps and extra fuel. She wore a leather aviator cap and heavy leather jacket for warmth, and her favorite scarf and special bracelet for luck. Her pockets held a compact make-up case and a small vial of smelling salts to use to wake herself up if she became drowsy on the 13 1/2 -hour flight. She opened canned tomato juice with an ice pick that also kept her windshield clear. Finally, in case of trouble, she had flares that she could light and toss out the window to communicate with other planes and ground crews in case of trouble.

Amelia's favorite scarf

Amelia's lucky bracelet

Make-up case

Smelling salts

Ice pick

Canned juice was easy to carry.

Flares of colored smoke were used to communicate with other planes and ground crews.

Fashion

For most people, high fashion was seen only in women's magazines or at the movies, in which elegant stars wore glamorous, well-cut, expensive clothing. Although most women and girls could never afford the dream dresses of the stars, they found all sorts of thrifty ways to squeeze a bit of style out of their tight budgets.

A 1930s fashion magazine

INAUGURAL OUTFIT
Eleanor Roosevelt wore this lilac velvet outfit to her husband's 1933 inauguration ceremony. A cross-over front and a *gored*, or slightly flared, skirt gave it the sleek, stylish lines that were popular in the 1930s.

CELEBRITY FASHIONS
In addition to her high-flying career as a pilot, Amelia Earhart, who favored a sleek, unfussy look, had her own clothing line for active women.

Amelia Earhart, pilot and dress designer

DELINEATOR

*Close-fitting hats were popular for girls and women. The **cloche** (klosh) hat got its name from its shape—the French word for "bell."*

Well-dressed movie stars Ginger Rogers and Fred Astaire danced their way through many 1930s movies—and influenced fashion as they did.

ACCESSORIES

A new collar and cuffs could spruce up an old dress. Women also used hats, shoes, and jewelry to update their wardrobes.

Lapel pins added a touch of sparkle and originality.

This google-eyed girl's pin was made from an early plastic called **Bakelite**.

Fancy shoes could make a simple outfit elegant.

SHIRLEY TEMPLE STYLE

Even child star Shirley Temple had a fashion statement to make. She wore short dresses in simple shapes that were easy to make at home. Women could buy the ready-made patterns and sew the dresses for their own daughters.

SHIRLEY TEMPLE IN "NOW AND FOREVER"

For dress-up, girls wore round-toed black shoes called "Mary Janes."

Feed-Sack Fashion

For farm families, fabric for making clothes was free if you didn't mind using the cloth sacks that had held flour and animal feed. Everything from dresses to bathing suits to underwear could be made from flour and feed sacks. In the early 1930s, these sacks were plain and white, printed with the name or trademark of the company that made the product inside. Later on, they came printed with animal, flower, and stripe designs. Sometimes families bought specific sacks of flour and feed just to get the prettiest ones!

These sisters are wearing matching feed-sack swimming suits made by their mother.

Girls wore what they had—and what their families could afford. As long at it was clean, any dress would do for a birthday party!

Putting America Back to Work

The new president, Franklin Delano Roosevelt, wasted no time in starting to tackle the Depression. His campaign pledge to deliver "a new deal for the American people" was followed up with action. In his first three months in office—known as the Hundred Days—President Roosevelt signed new bills into law that ended the nation's long banking crisis and created agencies to help the unemployed, bring electricity to rural areas, and help farmers. By the end of the Hundred Days, the Depression wasn't over, but the fear of it was.

President Roosevelt used the radio to tell Americans about many new programs and agencies that would help them. People began calling Roosevelt's programs the "alphabet soup programs" because so many were referred to by their initials. People even called the president by his initials—FDR!

These girls were eager to show their support of the NRA.

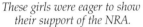

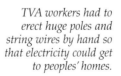

TURN ON THE LIGHTS!
Many rural areas of the United States did not have electricity in the 1930s. FDR created the Tennessee Valley Authority, or TVA, to do two things: to provide jobs and to bring electricity to the people of the Tennessee River Valley.

TVA workers had to erect huge poles and string wires by hand so that electricity could get to peoples' homes.

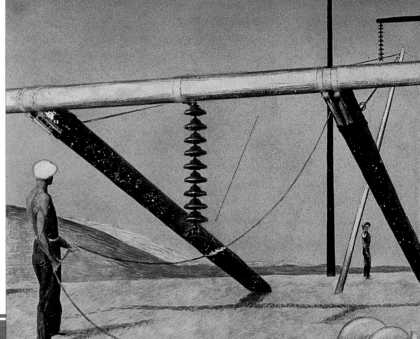

FLYING THE BLUE EAGLE
One goal of the National Recovery Act (NRA) was to raise wages for workers. Employers who promised to pay workers at least 40¢ an hour could display a poster with the NRA symbol on it—a blue eagle. Soon there were Blue Eagle posters on buses and billboards, encouraging shoppers to buy only at "Blue Eagle businesses."

One WPA program hired librarians to bring books to people who lived in the Appalachian Mountains, far from any library. These librarians packed up their saddlebags and went from house to house delivering books to grateful readers.

Works Progress Administration, or WPA, projects put men to work building and improving highways, bridges, and dams.

SAVING THE COUNTRY WITH THE CCC

Hundreds of thousands of Civilian Conservation Corps (CCC) recruits—like Kit's brother, Charlie—planted forests, built bridges, and took care of public land. In exchange, they got food, a place to sleep, and $30 per month—$25 of which they had to send home to their families. The CCC was one of the most popular New Deal programs—but women were not allowed to join!

Good Days, Bad Days

When the Depression hit West Virginia, Ruth Morrison's father was a *stonemason*, or builder, without a job. People weren't building any new houses, so there was no call for the sturdy fireplaces and chimneys Mr. Morrison took such pride in building. Mr. Morrison wasn't happy about accepting government help, but he signed up for WPA work so that he could feed his family. But even WPA jobs were uncertain and often only part-time. Some days or even weeks there was *no* work.

Ruth and her older sister, Evelyn, knew the moment they came in the door for lunch if their father had work or not. If his lunchbox was on the kitchen table, it was a bad day—another day without work. But if the lunchbox was gone, the girls knew it was a good day—a day when their dad had a job.

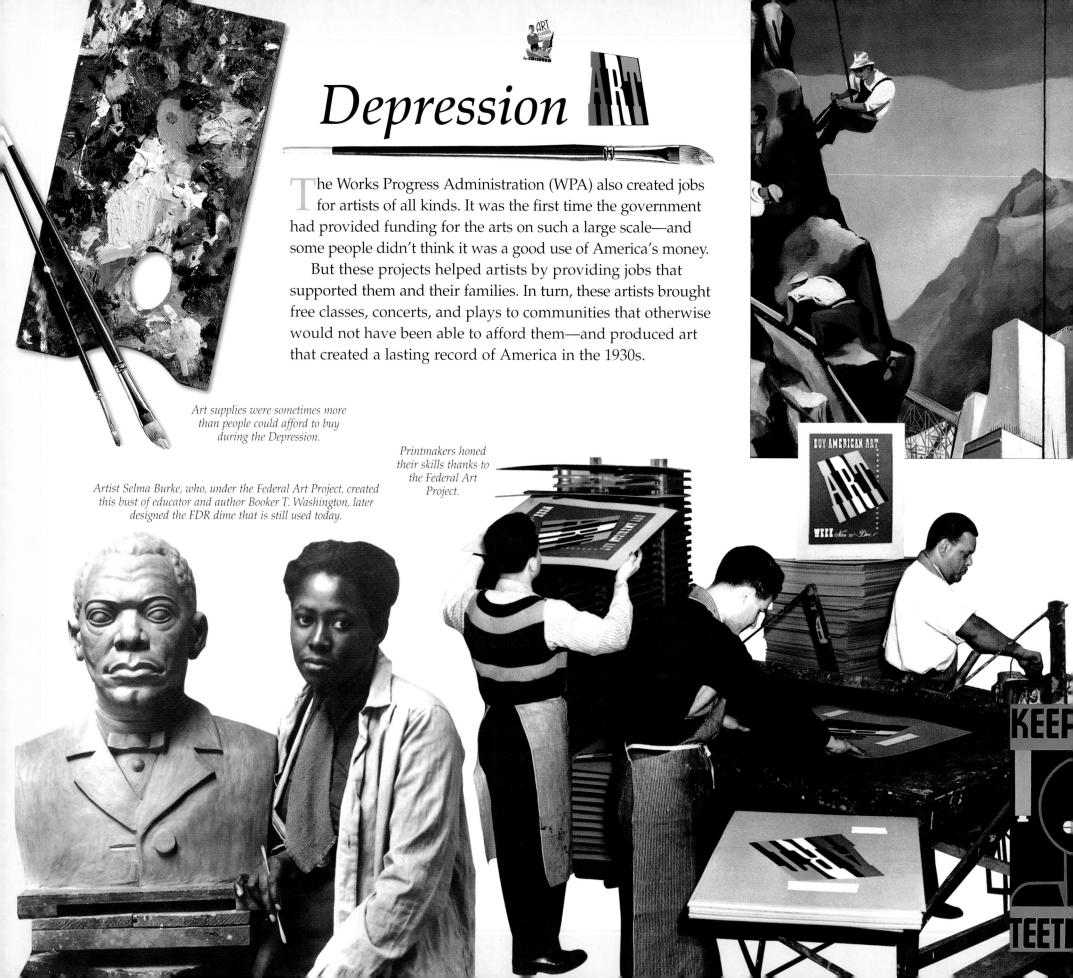

Depression ART

The Works Progress Administration (WPA) also created jobs for artists of all kinds. It was the first time the government had provided funding for the arts on such a large scale—and some people didn't think it was a good use of America's money.

But these projects helped artists by providing jobs that supported them and their families. In turn, these artists brought free classes, concerts, and plays to communities that otherwise would not have been able to afford them—and produced art that created a lasting record of America in the 1930s.

Art supplies were sometimes more than people could afford to buy during the Depression.

Artist Selma Burke, who, under the Federal Art Project, created this bust of educator and author Booker T. Washington, later designed the FDR dime that is still used today.

Printmakers honed their skills thanks to the Federal Art Project.

In post offices and public buildings, WPA artists painted dramatic murals, such as this 1937 mural showing the building of Hoover Dam. Many of these murals still exist today.

The Federal Theater Project produced all kinds of plays, from children's plays to Shakespearian comedies and dramas. Plays were performed for free in theaters, schools, and even outdoors in city parks.

FEDERAL THEATRE

PINOCCHIO

A DRAMATIC FANTASY FOR THE YOUNG IN HEART

COPLEY THEATRE

Beginning TUESDAY

FIVE NIGHTS WEEKLY TUES

ART CLASSES for CHILDREN

Some of the posters created under the Federal Art Project were used to promote public health and safety.

WPA artists went into cities and small towns to teach art to children.

OUR

LEAN

Documenting the Times

One of the New Deal programs that changed how people saw America—and themselves—was a large-scale photography project sponsored by the Farm Security Administration, or FSA. Dozens of FSA photographers traveled across America, taking pictures of what they saw. These and other documentary photographs were published in newspapers and magazines throughout the 1930s and created an important record of the Depression.

Many photographers focused on the faces of their subjects to show the spirit and determination of America.

New York City at Night

While FSA photographers set out to capture rural America on film, other photographers focused their lenses on the city. This photo shows how the new tall buildings called "skyscrapers" were changing the skylines of American cities.

Migrant Family

*Dorothea Lange's 1936 photographs of a **migrant**, or traveling, farm worker and her children inside their makeshift tent documented the desperation of homeless farm workers in California.*

FSA photographs showed Americans what was happening in the Dust Bowl.

Farm After Dust Storm

This close-up portrait of the family to the left was printed in magazines and newspapers across the country and became a famous symbol of the Depression and its miseries. Of this photograph, Lange later said, "There are moments such as these when time stands still. All you do is hold your breath and hope it will wait for you."

Dorothea Lange, FSA Photographer

Dorothea Lange knew she wanted to be a photographer long before she ever owned a camera. After achieving success as a portrait photographer, she spent most of the 1930s traveling and taking pictures of some of the poorest people in America. She tried in all her photographs to show not just how poor people were, but "their pride, their strength, their spirit."

Early professional cameras were bulky and heavy.

Standing on top of a car to take a photo, Lange pulled a camera **shroud** over her head. The dark cloth kept out light so she could see through the camera.

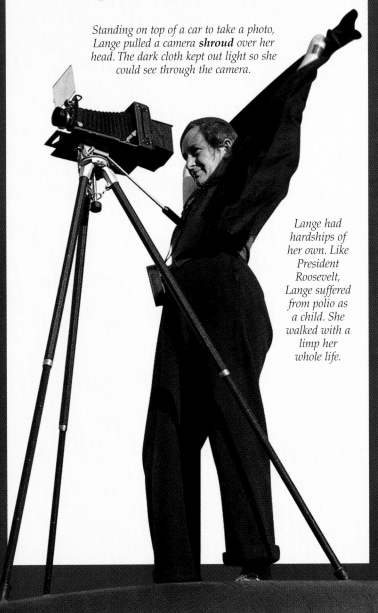

Lange had hardships of her own. Like President Roosevelt, Lange suffered from polio as a child. She walked with a limp her whole life.

On STRIKE!

The hardships of the Depression convinced many people that it was time to improve the lives of regular working people.

All over the country, in many different kinds of factories and businesses, employees began organizing into *unions*, or groups of workers who join together for a common goal. One person asking for a raise or shorter work hours could be ignored or even fired. But if 300 workers demanded those things, businesses would have to listen. If they didn't, the union would call a *strike*. Then nobody would work until an agreement was made. Many business leaders did not like being forced to meet workers' demands and fought the unions, sometimes even with violence.

Unions were not always successful in bringing about immediate change. But by sticking together, workers found strength and hope for the future.

Striking workers' families sometimes joined in the fight for better working conditions.

STRIKING TOGETHER
Organized protests brought together black workers and white workers in search of the same goals—more jobs, better pay, and better working conditions.

Textile factory workers went on strike in 1934 in one of the largest and most violent strikes America has ever seen. The government got involved to stop the violence, but in the end, the workers gained little.

Protesters often carried signs showing which side they supported.

Sit-Down Strikes

In late December 1936, workers in Flint, Michigan, planned and carried out a new kind of strike. Instead of working, they literally sat down inside a huge General Motors automobile plant. The *sit-down* strike soon spread to other General Motors plants in Michigan and completely disrupted the company.

The sit-down in Flint went on for 44 days. It ended only when General Motors agreed to recognize the United Auto Workers, or UAW, as the union that represented the auto workers. Most of the Flint auto workers were men. But that first sit-down strike would never have succeeded if not for women, and one woman in particular— Genora Johnson Dollinger.

On the night of December 30, police cut off the strikers' food supply and began throwing tear gas into the plant. The men were ready to give up— until Genora made a speech that was broadcast into the streets of Flint. "I'm talking especially to you women out there," she declared. "You didn't know that mothers are being fired on by the police. The police are cowards enough to fire into the bellies of unarmed men. Aren't they also cowards to fire at mothers of little children? I'm asking you women out there behind the barricades to break through these police lines. Come down here and stand with your brothers,

your sons, your sweethearts, your husbands, and help us win this fight."

And they did. A crowd of women walked through the barriers and into the plant, and the Women's Emergency Brigade

was born. The Emergency Brigade organized communication lines and ran first-aid stations. The women stood outside the plant with signs and sticks to make sure no company guards sneaked inside to stop the strike. Most of all, they inspired and encouraged the striking workers to keep going until they won.

Auto workers inside the plant during the 1936 sit-down strike

COPYCAT STRIKES
The sit-down labor strike seemed to be sweeping the country in 1937. Protesters of all kinds, such as these Detroit waitresses, tried it.

Symbols of H*pe

By the mid-1930s, people realized that tough times would be with them for a while. In the darkest days of the Depression, they looked for symbols of hope and better times ahead. They took strength from the bold actions of an energetic new president and his wife, the glimmer of Olympic success, the brilliance of amazing new inventions, and even the survival of five tiny baby girls.

In 1935, FDR created Social Security to provide workers with money when they retired. It is the only New Deal program still going today.

FIRESIDE HOPE
Families eagerly gathered around their radios to listen to President Roosevelt's "fireside chats." In these broadcasts, FDR told the country about new government programs designed to fight the Depression, and he reassured Americans that the country *would* survive the hard times and be prosperous and strong once again.

HER WAY
The First Lady kept in touch with Americans in her own way. She wrote a newspaper column called "My Day" that was printed in 180 newspapers nationwide. In it, she wrote about the people she met and the things she saw in Washington, D.C. and in her travels. Americans felt they were being heard—and felt hopeful.

Mrs. Roosevelt writing her column

My Day
By
ELEANOR ROOSEVELT

DES MOINES, Iowa, Monday.—A pleasant evening last night in Chicago talking to Mr. and Mrs. Charles Braested and Louis Ruppel.' I reached the train a little before 11 o'clock and arrived here at 7:30 this morning.
I cannot quite get accustomed to so much solicitude and on the part of everybody. Some day

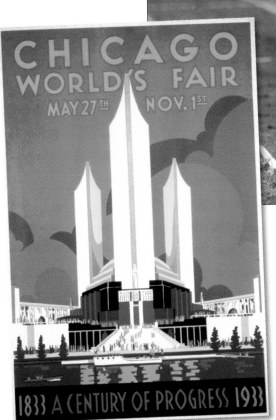

CHICAGO WORLD'S FAIR
MAY 27TH NOV. 1ST

1833 A CENTURY OF PROGRESS 1933

IN 193
THE NEW YORK WORLD'S FAIR

TWO WORLD'S FAIRS
In spite of the hard times, there were two well-attended world's fairs during the 1930s. In 1933, even families with little money to spare made the trip to Chicago to celebrate "A Century of Progress." In 1939, the New York fair gave a hopeful peek into the future—and a glimpse of such amazing new inventions as the television!

Girls collected
mementos, like
this fan, of the quints.

FARTHER AND FASTER

Mildred "Babe" Didrickson won two gold medals and a silver at the 1932 Los Angeles Olympic Games. Babe was only 21 when she broke the world records in the javelin toss and the 80-meter hurdles, and her achievements inspired girls everywhere.

UNLIKELY SURVIVORS

In 1934, five tiny baby girls were born in Canada. Together the identical Dionne quintuplets weighed less than 14 pounds. The whole world took hope from these unlikely survivors. Girls like Kit and Ruthie filled scrapbooks with photos of the "quints" doing everything from romping in the snow to visiting the Queen of England.

Breaking the Color Barrier

In 1939, Marian Anderson was a world-famous singer. She had performed for kings and queens in Europe and was the first African American ever invited to perform at the White House. But because of the color of her skin, a group called the Daughters of the American Revolution (DAR) refused to let Anderson perform at Constitution Hall in Washington, D.C.

Many people were outraged by this, including First Lady Eleanor Roosevelt. Instead, the government invited Anderson to sing on the steps of the Lincoln Memorial. On April 9, 1939, more than 75,000 people crowded together to hear her sing. The DAR got the message. Four years later, the group invited Marian Anderson to sing at Constitution Hall—and she did.

BACK TO WORK

The Depression started to come to an end when American factories started producing goods and supplies to help England and France fight Germany in World War Two. No one wanted to fight, but Americans were glad to have jobs.

A Peek into the Future

From the book *Changes for Kit*

Kit held the newspaper in her two hands and looked at her letter and photographs. Thousands of people would read this newspaper and see the photos of the hobo children. Thousands of people would read words that she had written.

—Valerie Tripp,
Changes for Kit

Kit learned many things during the tough times of the Depression: making do, staying cheerful, and the importance of pulling together. She also learned to open her heart to those most in need. These were the qualities that saw millions of Americans through more than ten long years of the Great Depression—years during which Americans' hope and optimism for the future were sorely tested.

Kit and her family survived the Depression, but they faced new hardships and sacrifices when America plunged into World War Two in 1941. In fact, it was the war that finally brought the Great Depression to an end. When America's factories geared up to make weapons and supplies to fight Germany, Americans had jobs once again.

Kit would have been 18 years old when America entered the war. Perhaps her talent for writing would have led Kit to become a war correspondent. Her stories might have helped Americans on the home front understand what was happening in the war—just like her letter to the editor in 1934 helped the people of Cincinnati understand the needs of the homeless children of the Depression.

When the war ended in 1945, America entered a peaceful, prosperous time. After more than 15 years of hardship, many Americans finally could own homes, have plenty to eat, and buy the things they wanted. Times were indeed better, but girls like Kit who lived through the Depression never forgot the hardships and lessons of the 1930s. The Great Depression had changed them—and America—forever.